Amelia Earhart

Judy Wearing

W WEIGL PUBLISHERS INC.
"Creating Inspired Learning"
www.weigl.com

Published by Weigl Publishers Inc.
350 5th Avenue, 59th Floor
New York, NY 10118
Website: www.weigl.com

Library of Congress Cataloging-in-Publication Data

Wearing, Judy.
 Amelia Earhart / Judy Wearing.
    p. cm. -- (My life)
 Includes index.
 ISBN 978-1-61690-059-5 (hardcover : alk. paper) -- ISBN 978-1-61690-060-1 (softcover : alk. paper) --
 ISBN 978-1-61690-061-8 (e-book)
 1. Earhart, Amelia, 1897-1937--Juvenile literature. 2. Women air pilots--United States--Biography--Juvenile literature. 3. Air pilots--United States--Biography--Juvenile literature. I. Title.
 TL540.E3W43 2010
 629.13092--dc22
 [B]

                                    2010005473

Printed in the United States of America in North Mankato, Minnesota
1 2 3 4 5 6 7 8 9 0 14 13 12 11 10

042010
WEP264000

Editor: Heather C. Hudak   **Design**: Kenzie Browne

Weigl acknowledges Getty Images as its primary image supplier for this title.

CONTENTS

Who is Amelia Earhart?

Amelia Earhart was a pilot in the early 1900s. This was soon after airplanes had been invented. Earhart became one of the world's best-known pilots. She earned many flying **records**.

Earhart wanted to be the first woman to fly around the world. She was trying to do this when her plane went missing in 1937.

Earhart and her **navigator**, Fred Noonan, were flying across the Pacific Ocean when their plane went missing.

Growing Up

Earhart was born in Atchison, Kansas, in 1897. She and her younger sister, Muriel, had many adventures. They collected insects, played games and sports, and read books.

Earhart's parents moved many times. Until she was 12, Earhart and her sister lived with their grandparents. Then, they moved to Iowa to be with their parents. Later, the girls moved with their mother to Chicago, Illinois. Earhart finished high school in 1915. After, she went to a **finishing school**. Earhart left school to work as a nurse's aide during World War I. Later, she went to college and became a **social worker**.

All About Kansas

- Kansas has four neighbors. They are Nebraska, Missouri, Colorado, and Oklahoma.
- Kansas became part of the **Union** in 1861.
- Wichita is the largest city in Kansas. It is known for its aircraft companies.

Kansas is nicknamed the "Sunflower State."

Influences

Earhart's mother, Amy, encouraged her daughters to chase their dreams. Amy supported her children if they wanted to do activities that were thought to be for boys only. In fact, she often dressed them in boys' clothes.

Earhart saw an airplane for the first time when she was 10 years old. More than 10 years passed before she decided to learn about flying. Earhart was taught by Anita "Neta" Snook. Snook was a female pilot who ran an **airfield**. The price for each lesson was $1 per minute in the air. Snook was a good teacher. Earhart did well as a student.

Practice Makes Perfect

In 1920, Earhart took her first plane ride. She knew right away that she wanted to be a pilot. Earhart started flying lessons less than a week later.

It took Earhart six months to save enough money to buy a plane. She called her plane *Canary* because it was yellow like the bird of the same name. At the time, people thought women should not fly planes. Earhart had to prove she could be a good pilot.

Earhart set her first flying record in 1922. She was the first woman to fly at a height of 14,000 feet (4,267 meters).

In 1928, Earhart joined two men as they flew across the Atlantic Ocean from Trepassey harbor, Newfoundland, to Burry Port, Wales. As a **passenger** on the flight, she was the first female to make the trip. Later, President Calvin Coolidge met the team at the White House. They celebrated the record.

In the 1920s, Earhart became the 16th woman to get a pilot **license**.

In 1932, Earhart became the first woman to fly **solo** across the Atlantic Ocean. She had planned to land in Paris. However, the weather was bad, and she had problems with her plane. Earhart had to land in Ireland instead.

In 1937, Earhart tried to fly around the world. Her plane took off from New Guinea to go to Howland Island. This part of the trip was 2,500 miles (4,023 kilometers). Earhart's plane ran out of fuel over the Pacific Ocean. She never arrived at Howland Island. Some people think Earhart's plane landed on another small island in the Pacific, called Nikumaroro. However, she was never found.

Overcoming Obstacles

As a child, Earhart's father was a lawyer for a railroad company. He had to move often. Earhart mostly lived with her grandparents. She rarely saw her father when she was young. Earhart would travel to visit him.

When Earhart became a pilot, few women worked outside the home. Most women married and stayed home to care for their children. As a woman, Earhart had to prove that she could be a good pilot. She kept newspaper stories about women who held jobs that were usually done by men. This encouraged Earhart to keep working hard.

Achievements and Successes

Earhart was the first woman and the second person in the world to fly across the Atlantic Ocean in a plane by herself. President Hoover awarded her the National Geographic Society's Gold Medal for her bravery.

Earhart was the first woman to make trips across the United States and North America by herself. She also worked with many organizations to help women become pilots.

Earhart married George P. Putnam in 1931.

Earhart set many world records. In 1930, she set a women's world record, flying 181.18 miles (291.58 km) per hour.

Earhart **designed** clothes for women. Her clothing line included blouses, pants, suits, dresses, and hats.

Earhart wrote two books about her experiences. The story of her 1928 flight across the Atlantic is called "20 Hrs., 40 Min." "The Fun of It" is her **autobiography**.

Earhart's childhood home is now a museum. The Amelia Earhart Birthplace Museum is found in Atchison, Kansas. People can tour the house and view photographs of Earhart's life. Maps show what may have happened during Earhart's last flight.

What is a Pilot?

A pilot is a person who flies an airplane. Orville and Wilbur Wright were the first pilots. They flew the first working airplane in 1903.

Pilots do more than just fly planes. They can also read flight maps and navigate the plane.

Pilots Through History

Like Earhart, these pilots set records and made flying history.

Harriet Quimby

Harriet Quimby was the first female pilot in the United States. Soon after getting her license in 1911, she flew from England to France. She died in a plane accident a few months later.

Charles Lindbergh

Charles Lindbergh was a U.S. pilot who set many records. In 1927, he flew in a plane alone across the Atlantic Ocean. He started his flight in New York City and landed in Paris.

Jacqueline "Jackie" Cochran

Jackie Cochran earned her pilot license in 1932. She had just three weeks of lessons. Cochran could fly faster and higher than any pilot at the time. She set many records.

Timeline

1920s | Earhart began taking flying lessons and later earned her pilot license.

1922 | Earhart broke the women's record for flying height. She flew 14,000 feet (4,267 m) above the ground.

1928 | Earhart became the first woman to fly across the Atlantic Ocean as a passenger on a plane. She wrote a book about the flight.

1930 | Earhart set two speed records for women pilots.

1932 Earhart became the first woman to fly across the Atlantic Ocean in a plane by herself. She wrote a book about the experience.

1935 Earhart became the first person to fly solo between Honolulu, Hawai'i, and Oakland, California.

1937 Earhart started a flight around the world. Her plane disappeared, and she was never found.

Write a Biography

A person's life story can be the subject of a book. This kind of book is called a biography. Biographies describe the lives of people who have had great success or done important things to help others. These people may be alive today, or they may have lived many years ago.

Try writing your own biography. First, decide who you want to write about. You can choose a pilot, such as Amelia Earhart, or any other person you find interesting. Then, find out if your library has any books about this person.

Write down the key events in this person's life.
- What was this person's childhood like?
- What has he or she accomplished?
- What are his or her goals?
- What makes this person special or unusual?

Answer the questions in your notebook. Your answers will help you write your biography review.

Find Out More

To learn more about Amelia Earhart, visit these websites.

This website includes photos of Earhart and information about her life.
www.ameliaearhart.com

Learn about Earhart's life and about other women pilots at this site.
www.ameliaearhartmuseum.org

See the journey Earhart tried to take around the world. Read her diary, and see photographs from the places she visited on this trip.
www.nauticalcurrents.com/
amelia_earhart_mem_flt.html

Try this quiz about Amelia Earhart.
www.kshs.org/kids/things/amelia

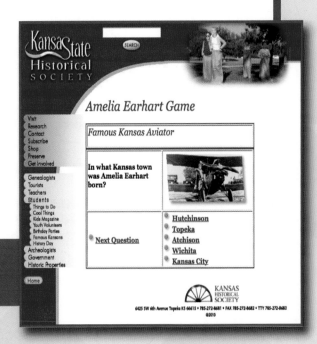

Glossary

airfield: a place where planes take off and land

autobiography: a book written by the person who is the subject of the story

designed: created something new

finishing school: a private school for girls to learn about culture and society

license: permission given to a person to fly or drive a vehicle

navigator: a person who uses maps and tools to plan a route

passenger: a person riding in a vehicle, such as a car, train, boat, or plane

records: top performances or achievements

social worker: a person who provides guidance and help to others

solo: to do a task alone

Union: states that joined together to form the United States

Index